Burmah

Burmah

A Photographic Journey

1855-1925

Noel F. Singer

Paul Strachan KISCADALE

Acknowledgements

I wish to thank Patricia Herbert for her enthusiastic and generous support. Grateful thanks also to Roser Flotats and Paul Strachan for giving me the opportunity of sharing these pictures with all who are interested in Burma.

This book is dedicated to Terence Blackburn, who over the years has with great patience accompanied me in my search for postcards and photographs.

Noel F. Singer
Bedfordshire, May 1993

PUBLISHED IN 1993 BY
PAUL STRACHAN - KISCADALE (LTD.)
GARTMORE, STIRLING FK8 3RJ

© NOEL F. SINGER
ISBN 1 870838 26 2

PRINTED IN ITALY BY GRAFICHE MILANI

Contents

Introduction: A Photographic Journey   7

    Rangoon   10

    The Shwe Dagon Pagoda   12

    Places of Interest   13

    Mandalay and the Palace   16

    The British in Upper Burma   17

    Monasteries and Pagodas   18

    Beyond Mandalay   19

    Burmese Beauties   20

    Festivals: Religious and Secular   21

    The Burmese Theatre   23

    Burmese Life   25

    Ethnic Groups   28

List of Photographers and Postcard Publishers   31

Bibliography   31

The Photographs   33

A Photographic Journey, 1855-1925　　　　မြန်မာ့ဓါတ်ပုံခရီး

I N BURMA, which is now called Myanmar, the early years of the Christian era saw the Pyu and the Mon, two of its oldest civilizations consolidate their respective kingdoms in the upper and lower coastal regions of the country. By the eleventh century, power had shifted into the hands of another ethnic group known as the Myanmar (Burmese), which is thought to have originated in Kansu, an area in the northwest of China.

Following this, and throughout Burma's long history, ethnic clashes have erupted, fragmenting the realm into petty kingdoms. Control of large areas was in turn enjoyed briefly by ambitious rulers from among the Burmese, Mon, Shan, and the Arakanese. In 1752, the Burmese again became dominant under Alaungphaya (r.1752-60), founder of the Konbaung Dynasty (1752-1885). The personalities of the autocratic and despotic rulers whose many titles included 'Lord of the Universe', were largely responsible for the swings in the fortunes of the country.

It was during the reigns of three ill-advised kings that clashes with the kingdom's giant neighbour, British India, occurred, resulting in the Anglo-Burmese Wars of 1825, 1852, and 1885. By 1852, the provinces along the sea coast had been annexed. Finally, in 1885 the whole country became part of the British Empire and was to become one of the more cherished gems in the imperial crown. After suffering hardships under the Japanese during the Second World War, Burma gained independence from Britain in 1948. At the time of writing the country is ruled by a military government.

This volume deals with the early days of colonial rule, circa 1895 to 1920, a progressive period when the country was known by many epithets, among them the Rice Bowl of Asia and the Land of Golden Pagodas. Burma's elegant daughters dressed in shimmering silks and shaded by pink parasols were the epitome of the Silken Ladies of the East.

The Burmese, together with a large number of ethnic minorities, are predominantly Buddhist, and the many thousands of pagodas can still be seen. Since earliest times Burmese men and women have poured their surplus wealth into religion, believing that this would bring merit, and was one of the ways of gaining admittance to the Buddhist version of heaven. Many of these activities took the form of building stupas, monasteries and commissioning an assortment of religious works of art. These monuments made excellent subjects for European photographers visiting the country. Foreign observers from the nineteenth century were astounded at the enormous amounts that the Burmese spent on religion, while the secular areas remained shabby. Until the 1880s the only outstanding buildings in the country, apart from the palace, were religious.

The Victorian visitors, filled with their own sense of superiority, and accustomed to the servility of the Indian, were surprised at the independent nature of the Burmese. They found the gilded shrines overpoweringly exotic, and smiled indulgently at the cheerful pilgrims in their brightly coloured silken clothes. The diversity of scenic settings, and the different costumes worn by minor ethnic groups, of which there are still believed to be over sixty, also amused them — it was all 'very quaint' and 'utterly charming'. As more Europeans began to take up residence from the 1880s, some enterprising foreigners grasped the opportunity to exploit in the form of photographs and post cards the country's unusual visual attractions.

Austria is credited with being the first country in the world to produce these post cards, which were issued by the Austrian Postal Authority on the lst October, 1869. They proved popular, since a card could be sent at half the cost of a letter. But it required the invention of photography to popularise the post card as a means of recalling scenes of foreign cultures, people, and events.

The birth of photography came about in January 1839 when Louis Daguerre (1789-1851) in France, and William Fox Talbot (1800-77) in England, announced their process of 'taking pictures from nature'. It was the latter who discovered the technique of reproducing prints from an original negative. Soon, post cards began to appear with a photograph pasted on one side. This type was believed to have been introduced into Burma by the Italian photographer, Felice A. Beato, in the 1890s. It soon paved the way for the printed versions illustrated in this book. Although it is not known when the first printed post card was used in Burma, it can be assumed that it was sometime during the second half of the 1890s; the earliest example in the author's collection is dated 24th July 1899.

A chronological sequence of photographs connected with Burma would probably begin in 1852 when John MacCosh, an army surgeon and one of the first British war photographers, recorded scenes of the Second Anglo-Burmese War. Examples of some of his work can be seen in a book by George Bruce, entitled *The Burma Wars*, others, are to be found in the National Army Museum at Chelsea in London, together with an astonishing collection of albums containing photographs taken by military personnel stationed in the country.

The next photographer of note was Captain Linneaus Tripe (1822-1902), who accompanied Henry Yule to the court of Mindon (r.1853-78) in 1855. Tripe photographed scenes of Rangoon and places of interest along the Irrawaddy River. However, his historically important photographs were those taken in and around Amarapura. Bearing in mind the difficulties involved in taking photographs at that time with heavy and primitive equipment, the results are nothing less than stunning. In Britain, Tripe's unique pictorial documents can be viewed at the British Library (Orbit House), the Victoria and Albert Museum, and at the Royal Photographic Society in Bath. In his pictures the glories of the palace city, which had once been compared to the abode of the gods, had long faded, and we see dilapidated pavilions and overgrown vegetation. The only buildings of architectural interest are the monasteries, with their intricately carved and gilded exteriors. Yule wondered how a race 'so deficient in all domestic appliances could be capable of designing or executing such exquisite workmanship'. Sadly, these magnificent structures have now all vanished.

Our Trip to Burmah (1875) by C. A. Gordon contained photographs pasted onto the pages. Many were by the photographers Jackson, Shepherd, Bourne, and Nicholas of Calcutta. They were probably the earliest professionals who visited Burma (sometime during the late 1860s and early 1870s) and built sets to photograph the 'natives' in their finery.

Another famous photographer was Peter Klier of Moulmein. It is not known when he arrived in the country but an engraving based on one of his

photographs appeared in *The Graphic* in March 1877. Klier had an eye for the unusual and many religious ruins which would have been ignored by another were fortunately immortalized by him. By the turn of this century he had joined the swelling ranks of post card producers.

Felice Beato, the Italian photographer and entrepreneur, who arrived in Burma soon after the fall of Mandalay in 1885, opened a studio and a curio shop in the city. The Raj tourist who visited Beato's premises was presented with a wide choice of photographs from a carefully prepared index. Copies of the selected pictures were later sent pasted in an album, with the title and negative number neatly written in pencil. A photographic catalogue of the handicrafts available in his shop could also be ordered through the post.

The post cards which were on sale at the Beato studios consisted of photographs mounted on cardboard, some with 'Wishing you a Happy New Year' printed on them. These cards were available from his shops at Mandalay and Rangoon, and were obviously intended to be sent through the post.

New Year Greeting Card, Mandalay. Beato, 1890s.

post. Beato was a businessman and knew instantly if a view was saleable. Scenes of architectural and cultural interest, together with 'curious' religious and secular ceremonies, which have long since been abandoned were fortunately photographed by him and Klier. Cynics may say that their cameras were only used to further their business interests, but were it not for these two photographers a way of life that has now disappeared would have been lost forever.

Many authors who travelled in Burma between 1890 and 1900 illustrated their books with photographs bought from Beato and Klier. In G.W. Bird's *Wanderings in Burma*, published in 1897, they were both included in a list of prominent photographers of Rangoon; the other three were Jackson and Co., Watts and Skein, and Khundan-Dass and Co.

Two other well known names, in Upper Burma, were Johannes of Mandalay, and S.N. Samuel, who once worked for Beato. There were even Japanese photographers setting up shop in Mandalay and Rangoon. One was Yamada and Co., and the other the Banzai Brothers. The two leading departmental stores in Rangoon, Rowe and Co., and Whiteaway, Laidlaw and Co., also produced lavishly illustrated picture books. These publications are now invaluable as historical documents, as many of the Victorian and Edwardian public buildings which survived the bombs of Second World War were demolished by the Government in the 1970s and 1980s; the official view being that the presence of these structures was a constant irritant and a shameful reminder that the proud Burmese (who had a habit of invading and subjugating adjacent countries) had themselves been conquered. It seemed that many of the splendid buildings, an exotic mixture of English, Indian, and Italian architecture, symbolized the 'wicked' colonial past.

Perhaps the most famous, certainly the most prolific producer of post cards which were mostly printed in Germany, was the Indian-owned company called Ahuja of Rangoon, who bought the rights to many of the best photographs produced in Burma around the turn of the century. A large number of the photographs, for Ahuja's early series, were acquired by them from the studios of Beato soon after his death in 1904; they then claimed copyright.

As the influx of European tourists increased and the demand for post cards grew, many of the photographers from whom Ahuja bought their material began producing their own. These were printed in such diverse places as Bavaria, Britain, India, Japan, and Saxony. The post cards, which were available from the Japanese companies in the 1920s were quite often labelled in a pidgin English that was unintentionally amusing. The titles, too,

could often be misleading.

Among the native Buddhist population pictures of a religious nature, such as the Tooth of the Buddha from Kandy in Sri Lanka, famous images, shrines and eminent ecclesiastics were eagerly sought. Brightly tinted post cards of celebrated male and female dancers were also extremely popular.

Collectors are usually interested in the visual aspect of the post card, but there is more to the card; one can also study printing techniques, the varieties in design, and the postmarks; the latter can fetch very high prices among enthusiasts. Post cards are immensely useful as a source of reference. Researchers are at last begining realized the significance of these little pieces of coloured card as important historical and social documents.

It is hoped that by turning the pages of this volume the reader will be transported back to a time when many of Burma's architectural wonders, such as the carved and gilded monasteries, decorated with multi-coloured glass mosaic, were still standing, when the national costumes of the diverse variety of the ethnic groups were brilliantly exotic, and when the only leisurely way up country was either on one of the splendid paddle steamers of the famous Irrawaddy Flotilla Company, or in the First Class compartment of the Burma Railways.

To visit places of interest, sightseers would have had to use either a pony, a horse carriage, or a delicately carved bullock cart, jingling with bells. Among ruined monasteries, and in particular, in the ancient city of Pagan with its 'myriad' pagodas, the tourist would have found neglected works of religious art lying there for the taking. Many did, and it is to these early souvenir hunters, whose 'mementos' make up most of the collections in the national museums in the United Kingdom, that we owe a great debt of gratitude. Sadly, the Burmese of the day had no interest or pride in the preservation and conservation of their antiquities. Were it not for the Raj tourists of the day, the existence of many of the objects which are now taken for granted in the national museums in Britain would never have been known.

Although late nineteenth-century photographs are believed to exist in the Universities' Central Library in Rangoon, very few post cards from the colonial period have survived, the three main hazards being destruction by fire (still a major threat as the majority of houses are of bamboo and timber), insects and climatic conditions (mildew, during the monsoon season). So much, too, was lost following air raids by the Americans, the British, and the Japanese during the Second World War.

According to information received from friends in the country, many modern-day Burmese are unaware of the existence of these early photographs. It is to be hoped that the publication of this work will remedy the situation. Young Burmese will probably see for the very first time the tranquil times of their great grandparents, when the sun cast a mellow haze upon gleaming pagodas and beautiful silken ladies [86].

Rangoon

At the turn of this century, a visitor entering British Burma on a steamer belonging to either the Bibby or the Henderson Line swept past vast paddy fields and tiny villages along the 21-mile stretch of the Rangoon River. His eyes would have been drawn to a bright golden spot in the distance. This beacon on a hill was the Shwe Dagon Pagoda, which still stands as an exotic backdrop to the city.

Along the river-front elephants retrieved huge teak logs from the water, and methodically stacked them in front of the saw-mills of the timber companies. These great patient beasts and their Indian riders were soon to be replaced by machinery.

In the heart of the city Europeans, Indians and Chinese thronged the pavements. The last two groups lived in their own communities, which were identifiable by the architecture of their houses, and places of worship. The Burmese and the Europeans were to be found mainly in the leafy suburbs.

For the visitor, the only structure in central Rangoon which indicated that he had arrived in the capital of Buddhist Burma was the 152-foot high Kyak Athok (Sule) Pagoda. As if to prove that this was a tolerant cosmopolitan city, close to this gilded shrine were the delicate minarets of a mosque, an American Baptist church, and an elaborately decorated Hindu temple to the elephant-headed god Ganesa, patron of traders. The now destroyed Town Hall, fronted by massive columns and ornamented with the figures of Mercury (the Roman god of merchants) and sundry other gods and goddesses, dominated this quarter. In the tree-lined streets, busy with trams, rickshaws and horse-drawn carriages, many of the pedestrians could be seen in their national costume [33].

The now bustling city was originally a Mon fishing village, but gained prominence in the fourteenth century. It is mentioned in Mon inscriptions either as Tigumpanagara or Lagun, in association with the Buddhist shrine Kyak Lagun on the summit of the hill. The word Lagun was later corrupted by the Burmese to Dagon, and the stupa came to be known as the Shwe Dagon (Golden Dagon) [38].

Government House, Rangoon.

In 1757, the name of the town was changed by Alaungphaya (r.1752-60) to Yangon (End of Threat), after he had crushed the Mon kingdom of Hamsawati, with its capital at Bago (Pegu). Until 1852, the little port was stockaded, the houses mean and shoddily built. This probably conformed to the Burmese sumptuary laws in existence at the time, only the ruling elite being allowed large wooden houses. The land was marshy and parts of it subject to flooding at high tide.

Soon after the Second Anglo-Burmese War of 1852, the British in turn anglicized Yangon to Rangoon. Their engineers, accompanied by demolition teams, completely razed the whole area to make way for substantial brick and wooden houses. It was a boom time for the building industry, and by 1900 many hotels and public buildings had been erected. Regrettably, nothing now remains of old Lagun, and the few Mon pagodas that escaped being demolished have all been renovated in a modern Burmese style.

The premier place of interest for the Raj tourist was the Shwe Dagon Pagoda, its circular platform crowded with gilded shrines of the most extravagant design. In the evenings, one could stroll in the beautifully laid out public gardens, and listen to the military bands, or drive, or row around the placid Royal Lakes. The famous clubs, such as the Gymkhana, and the Pegu (both out of bounds to non-Europeans) offered excellent service and pampered their members in genteel surroundings [70].

Whiteaway, Laidlaw & Co., Ld., Rangoon.

An evening of Western style entertainment could usually be found at the Jubilee Hall. Plays and variety shows were provided either by local British amateur dramatic societies, or by touring companies from Europe and England. The latter usually appeared during the cool season (October to February) after a tour of India. By 1900, Rangoon had been completely transformed and was unrecognizable from the insignificant little port of the early 1850s [34].

The largest concentration of Burmese, referred to as 'Jack Burman' by the English, were to be found in Kemmindine, west of Rangoon. Here lived rich merchants, craftsmen, petty traders, and the people from the world of entertainment. The area east of the Shwe Dagon Pagoda also supported a Burmese community. This section of the capital was usually thronged with pilgrims ascending and descending the covered stairway leading to the platform of the great pagoda, or visiting the large clusters of wooden monasteries at the base of the hill.

When performing their religious duties at a shrine, the Burmese always dress in their best clothes. The rich colours, the jewels of the beautifully made up ladies, with coronets of flowers in their hair and silk shawls floating around them, must have stopped many a Raj tourist in his tracks.

Throughout the year, either on the vast platform of the Shwe Dagon, or in the surrounding streets below, various Buddhist festivals are celebrated.

Whether solemn or exuberant, a procession was usually accompanied by dancers and musicians. Gaily dressed worshippers carrying offerings and gold umbrellas, or excitedly surging around fantastically shaped beasts made out of paper, tinsel and bamboo filled the crowded avenues.

The Chinese, or 'John Chinaman', were allocated a quarter in West Rangoon. There, complete with several impressive joss houses, rampant with glazed dragons, members of this hard-working race lived in tall tightly packed brick buildings and became valued members of the community.

Although it was common for a Chinese male to take a Burmese wife, a Burman rarely married a Chinese. In a mixed marriage only male children were brought up according to Chinese tradition, the girls were considered Burmese and dressed in the costume of their mother. Occasionally, theatrical troupes from China or Singapore visited the community. The performers, robed in ornate costumes, must have been an impressive sight, although it is doubtful whether the story line and the dialogue of the opera could be followed by many of the Sino-Burmese. China Town, too, had its own amateur dramatic societies. These were noticeable by the strange mixture of partly Burmese and Chinese costumes worn by the lesser characters. Ahuja, the post card company, ran a series on Chinese Beauties who were dressed in both the latest fashions, and in the traditional way. These cards were sold in many of the Chinese-owned shops throughout the country.

Almost all of the races of India were to be found in Rangoon. Just as hard working as the Chinese, many were merchants who became extremely wealthy and owned large tracts of fertile land in the Delta. In a post card entitled 'Rice Merchants of Rangoon', only Indians can be seen. Lower Burma soon attracted huge numbers of cheap Indian labourers, who undercut the easygoing and tolerant Burmese, many of whom found themselves heavily in debt to the Indian money lenders. Thus began the tensions which were to have disastrous consequences in the riots of 1930.

The business centre of this thriving Indian community was Moghul Street, with its prominent white mosque [35]. Like the Chinese, Indians also brought in their own entertainment. Ahuja also printed a series on Indian Beauties, together with coy pictures of the celebrated female entertainers of the day. Another set of post cards which was popular were the garishly coloured paintings of the Hindu gods and goddesses. These were no doubt aimed at the thousands of Indian coolies who were to be found in almost all the larger towns and cities. Until about 1920, any procession or festival taking place in central Rangoon was invariably of either Chinese or Indian origin.

There were a few Japanese companies in the city, and although the men sometimes brought their families with them, their community was not large. It seems that they kept a low profile, and traded in general goods and Japanese works of art. Many of their shops also included a photographic studio. It was whispered that there were Japanese brothels in Rangoon and Mandalay.

From reading books of the period, the impression is gained that between 1880 and 1910, many of the colonials got on extremely well with the Burmese. For the thakin and the thakinma, the Burmese equivalent of the sahib and the memsahib, those were indeed the Golden Days. Surrounded by obsequious Indian servants, they looked down benignly on the 'sons and daughters of the Empire', and were either charmed or irritated by their quaint ways. But thereafter, many of the young administrators and their wives who arrived in the country adopted aloof and patronizing attitudes. Indian office workers were preferred to Burmese, which naturally caused intense resentment.

The leading departmental stores offered to the English and European communities all the comforts of life from home. By 1910, they were also publishing beautifully presented albums of picturesque scenes, and photographs of the diverse inhabitants of the highlands.

Apart from a few specialist establishments, Burmese crafts were rarely stocked or given prominence in the curio shops, which were usually run by foreigners. The preferred objects were either Chinese, Indian or Japanese. A well travelled and informed souvenir hunter usually waited until he was somewhere up country, where Burmese works of art could be acquired sometimes for free.

Meanwhile, there was much to see. The best time to meander around the broad shady streets was either in the morning or late afternoon. A horse-drawn carriage was always available to take one anywhere in the city.

The Shwe Dagon Pagoda

An old Mon chronicle states that the Buddha gave eight hairs to the brothers Phussa and Bhandika who, on their return to Burma from India, enshrined the relics in a jewelled cave beneath the pagoda. During the second half of the fifteenth century, the sanctity of the site spread and drew pilgrims from the surrounding Buddhist countries. Unfortunately, being in the earthquake belt, the structure has been badly damaged over the centuries. Successive rulers, both Mon and Burmese, repaired the pagoda and raised its height each time. Its present height of 326 feet was the work of the Burmese King Sinbyushin (r.1763-76) who came with his court to Rangoon in 1775. The act of rebuilding the pagoda was intended to acquire much needed merit after his invasions of several countries, which caused the deaths of thousands. However, he also had the last of the Mon rulers and his followers killed as he embarked on his religious devotions.

The Shwe Dagon is the second tallest religious structure in the country, the Shwe-maw-daw Pagoda (or in Mon Kyak Mah Tau), another Mon shrine in Pegu, being the highest at 373 feet.

James Alexander, in his *Travels from India to England* (1827), said that there were several thousand small pagodas in Rangoon, and that these had all been vandalized by British troops during the war of 1825. Apparently, the lure of the treasures hidden within the relic chambers had been too much for the men. The greatest concentration of pagodas was said to have been along the main road, or pilgrim's way, which ran from the river to the Shwe Dagon. At the time, a group led by a Major Fraser tunnelled 100 feet into the base of the Shwe Dagon, hoping to find a fabulous cave with its floor covered

Group of Japanese Ladies, Rangoon. Ahuja, c.1900.

three feet deep in gems. By the second half of 1860, all the desecrated shrines had been demolished by the British to make way for housing; only six large stupas were spared.

The tourist had a choice of four stairways to the summit of the hill on which the Shwe Dagon was built. At the top could be found shrines and temples of every description. Two bells of enormous size could also be seen. Burmese bells, unlike those made in the West, do not have a tongue and therefore cannot be rung, instead they are sounded with a wooden rod.

Once on the platform the sound of bells filled the air. They signalled the conclusion of a prayer, with the pilgrims making sure that the good spirits heard them and took note. From the jewel-encrusted finial of the Shwe Dagon would come chimes from hundreds of gold and silver bells. A group of girls could often be seen posturing to music provided by an orchestra, while in a nearby pavilion monks chanted Pali prayers. Elsewhere, flower sellers called attention to their freshly prepared bouquets.

Old prints and photographs of the vast platform show very little in the way of buildings, but between 1875 and 1910 small shrines and prayer halls began to mushroom around the base of the Shwe Dagon. These structures embody a time of plenty for the Burmese nouveaux riches, many of whom traded in rice and timber. Having become wealthy the donors vied with one another to produce the most extravagantly designed shrines. The platform rapidly became a storehouse of the best and very worst examples of Burmese crafts. Older buildings with restrained but exquisitely carved panels and roof ornaments were pulled down to make way for these new pavilions with their bewildering profusion of decorations [38]. Entire structures were intricately carved, lavishly gilded and set with thousands of coloured pieces of glass. But soon, wood was to give way to sheets of tin, as it was cheaper and easier to cut into shape; the surface, when lacquered, was then set with glass mosaic. Provided it was kept rust free, tin also lasted longer.

A visitor driving up from central Rangoon to the pagoda would use the southern stairs, the entrance of which was guarded by two lions, built in 1887[37]. Then as now, signs warned in several languages that shoes had to be removed before the ascent. But the sight of diseased beggars, many of them lepers with the disconcerting habit of spitting red betel juice, must have un-nerved many a foreigner. The thought of walking shoeless on the germ-infested steps probably stopped some tourists from experiencing the sights on the summit. A few hardy souls did make the climb wearing shoes, ignoring the outraged stares and remarks of the worshippers.

Shrine on Platform of the Shwe Dagon Pagoda, Rangoon. P. Klier

Rows of stalls selling curios, toys and musical instruments filled each side of the stairs. As the summit was approached one would have seen flower-sellers with mounds of exotic blooms, umbrellas of all sizes and flags, some of them made of gold, silver and coloured paper. Offerings brought by pilgrims were placed in a repository, its contents soon growing into a curious mixture of the incongruous, the paltry and the precious.

Roads from the east stairway led to many of the wooden monasteries of Bahan, and then on to the Zoological and Botanical Gardens and the Royal Lakes — the best point from which to view the Shwe Dagon was across its placid surface. From here, of an evening, could be seen the great golden stupa brightly lit against a glorious sunset.

Places of Interest

Before venturing north and into the interior, the traveller could visit towns and villages in the Delta region which had become famous either for their unique shrines, crafts, or memorable incidents in history.

East of Rangoon is the now tranquil old port of Syriam, which had been held in the seventeenth century by a Portugese adventurer named Philip De Brito. A plunderer of relic chambers, he paid for his sacrilegious acts by being impaled by Anaukphetlun (r.1605-1628) in 1613. Many a bloody battle

A Burmese *Hnaw* on the Irrawaddy.

was fought among the now ancient trees and tiny pagodas. A few miles out, on the road to Kyauk-tan, can be found the remains of the old Mon city of Pada; its ruined walls shaped in the form of a human foot. The city is believed to have been sacked in the eleventh century by the Burmese King Aniruddhadeva (r.1044-1077).

Pegu, to the north of Rangoon, would certainly have drawn the visitor. Although it was once the capital of a Mon kingdom, it is now a predominantly Burmese city; many of the original inhabitants having fled into Thailand to escape Burmese persecution in the eighteenth and nineteenth centuries. Here, too, many a battle had been enacted and much cruelty suffered by the people. The city rises out of the rice fields like a green island crowned by the tapering Shwe-maw-daw Pagoda, its gilded surface shining brightly in the sun. Foreign goods as well as local products could be seen in the stalls along the stairways and lining the busy main road leading to the shrine.

To the south-west of Pegu, four gigantic figures still rear their huge heads over the treetops. These are the Kyak Pan Buddhas, built by the Mon King Bana U (r.1348-1383) and which have now been irretrievably restored in the decadent Burmese style of the early 1900s. Such was the devastation wrecked on Pegu by the troops of Alaungphaya in 1757 that another now famous site known as the Shwe-thar-ly-aung (in Mon, Kyak Mahabuddharup) an

enormous reclining Buddha, became overgrown with vegetation and was only rediscovered in 1882 [43]. At the turn of this century, apart from a few well maintained pagodas, the rest, numbering several hundred scattered around the former capital, bore witness to the mindless vandalism perpetrated by man. It would seem that the temptation to pillage the relic chambers of stupas was not confined to non Buddhists.

Moving towards Thaton, another old and even earlier Mon city, an intrepid traveller would have had to brave the thick jungle paths and slippery slopes, to reach the unusual Kyaik-hti-yo Pagoda, built on a large boulder perched on the very edge of an abyss. The entire structure can still be rocked back and forth to the apprehension of the onlookers. It was once claimed that the rock actually hovered several inches off the ground, a miraculous phenomenon believed in implicitly by the faithful. The area was home to the tiger, the wild elephant and the ferocious rhinoceros. Simple folk believed that the local malevolent spirits were capable of harassing the unwary. A prudent pilgrim, therefore, made offerings at the little shrines along the way and propitiated these tormented beings.

Thaton, known of old as Raksapura, the City of Demons, is also renowned for its pagodas, religious objects of antiquarian interest, and spirit cults. King Aniruddhadeva is said to have attacked the city in 1057, and deported thousands of its inhabitants to Pagan.

Further south is the old port of Martaban, once famed for the ceramic jars which were shipped all over the Orient. On the opposite bank can still be seen the 'Old Moulmein Pagoda' visited by Kipling, and which is mentioned in his 'Road to Mandalay'. Moulmein was a gentle town, with a large number of European inhabitants living in impressive wooden houses set within spacious grounds. The town was also noted for the superb ivory carvings which were made for the Rangoon market. In the environs are to be found limestone caves; these were the haunts of tourists and pilgrims alike. Even as late as 1910, some of the caverns still held thousands of antique religious works of art, the offerings of Mon devotees over the centuries. Many have now been looted.

Returning to Rangoon, a traveller heading for the interior, and with time to spare, would have taken a cabin on one of the Irrawaddy Flotilla Company steamers. The busy towns of the delta, such as Twante and Bassein, were also accessible. Having navigated the creeks, the haunt of voracious crocodiles and clouds of mosquitoes, the steamer entered the Irrawaddy River, past towns and villages glinting with gold or white pagodas and sheltering among shady trees. Readers of the numerous accounts of the three Anglo-Burmese Wars probably found these bustling places of some interest as many had seen not inconsiderable action.

Prome, a large town dominated by the Shwe-san-daw Pagoda, provided the opportunity for observing the production of some of the traditional Burmese crafts, such as gold lacquerware and decorative pottery. At the ruined Pyu city of Sri Kshetra, situated nearby, the amateur archaeologist could pick up artifacts dating from before the eighth century.

Travelling further up the river, a dry landscape now replaced the familiar green hills and leafy villages. Thorn trees, and toddy palms grew in profusion. Past river side towns with their carved monasteries and mat houses and further up still, the great glowering bulk of Mount Popa, a huge extinct volcano, would have come slowly into view in the east, indicating to the traveller that Pagan was about to be reached.

This city of pagodas rose in the eleventh century, its crowded streets and lanes, used to staid religious and courtly processions, were to witness the thundering hoards of Kublai Khan's armies in 1287. Much has been written about the unguarded shrines and temples, with their precious contents. Art thieves were already homing in from the West and in 1899 objets d'art and wall paintings were stolen and removed to Germany; the thieving continues today.

Back on the placid Irrawaddy, rafts of teak logs or large floating platforms of bamboo to which were secured ceramic jars, could often be met with, seemingly heading straight for the paddle steamer. These potentially dangerous encounters were deftly avoided by the captain. There was, too, the risk of being stranded on a hidden sandbank. The river in spate could turn ferocious, carrying trees, or huge boats ripped from their moorings. Other hazards were sudden squalls and flash floods from the hills, which caused treacherous currents.

Past Pagan, the landscape gradually becomes flat and dreary, with little of interest to relieve the monotony. Further up the river, the appearance of the enormous white dome of the Kaung-hmu-daw Pagoda would have been greeted with relief. Sagaing, with its long range of hills, crowded with shrines and monasteries now beckoned, offering the tourist a choice of many a novel sight. In the distance, the high Shan mountains indicated that Mandalay was only a few miles away.

But first, the old city of Inn Wa, or Ava, had to be passed. Foreign

The Kyak Pan Buddhas, Pegu. P. Klier.

Kyaik-hti-yo Pagoda, Thaton. Ahuja.

observers of the eighteenth and nineteenth centuries have left accounts of the dazzling regattas which were held during the heyday of Ava's glory. They were impressed by the large number of gilded boats, canoes, and the exotically carved state barges of the Burmese royal family. Rowers sang as they manoeuvred their war canoes in complex patterns. Apart from the numerous pagodas and crumbling city walls, very little now remains of this once royal city.

Another striking feature in this area is the Shwe-kyet-yet Pagoda, with its cluster of dazzling white attendant stupas [48]. It is built on a steep cliff near the former capital of Amarapura, or City of Immortals. Tradition has it that Buddha, in a previous incarnation as a rooster, choose this spot to rest, but was disturbed and forced to move by the noise of the whirlpools and waves of the turbulent river. The Shwe-kyet-kya Pagoda on the next hillock marks the site of his new home; both shrines are said to date from the tenth century.

The river banks which only a few a few miles downstream were devoid of life and vegetation, became crowded with houses, monasteries and plantations. River traffic also increased as Mandalay was approached.

Mandalay and the Palace

Although archaeological excavations have not yet been carried out on Mandalay Hill, it is likely that, because of its prominence, it was used by man since ancient times. One of the earliest kings to be associated with the hill was Aniruddhadeva who built a stupa on the summit on his return from an expedition to Yunnan. However, the area sprung into prominence only during the following century, when Jeyasura I (r.1113-1160) exiled his son Minshinzaw to this region. The prince is said to have worked off his frustration by successfully transforming the wilderness for cultivation by creating reservoirs and canals.

For centuries, the land on which Mandalay now stands consisted mainly of paddy fields and tiny villages. This idyllic scene changed dramatically in 1857 when Mindon (r.1853-1878) decided to abandon the old city of Amarapura and build a new capital. His plan was no doubt triggered off by events in British Burma. Rangoon, the capital, was being transformed at an amazing speed by its new rulers, and Mindon felt that a similar action was also called for in his kingdom.

An 'ancient legend', fabricated to attract pilgrims, was 'discovered' which claimed that Buddha, accompanied by five hundred disciples, wafted through the air from India to the top of Mandalay Hill and predicted that a great city would rise in the nineteenth century. A young demoness, standing nearby, was overcome with piety and decided to cut off her breasts, offering them to the Holy One, who thereupon said that she would be reincarnated as the founder of the future city; it is not recorded if the gruesome gifts were accepted.

Mindon used the story as one of the reasons for the transfer of his capital, and in the process had the wooden palace buildings, and some of the carved monasteries from Amarapura, dismantled and re-erected at the new site. A rumour was also circulated to the effect that those who lived within the shadow of the hill would enjoy the blessing of longevity. Despite another 'ancient' prophesy which claimed that a long line of kings were destined to rule, only two sovereigns were to enjoy this privilege.

Mandalay, or to give it its classical name, Yadanapon (Mound of Jewels), was formally inaugurated in 1859. The palace, which consisted of a collection of buildings, was defended by a huge stockade of teak pillars. This was further enclosed by a wall beyond which lived the princes, officials, and retainers. They, in turn, were protected by another square brick wall and moat.

The royal residence was dominated by a structure with seven diminishing roofs, beneath which was the principal hall of audience and the Lion Throne [50, 51]. It was to this vast chamber that the officials of the kingdom came, three times a year, to pay homage to the monarch and his chief queen. To the north of the palace were pleasure gardens with canals and rustic bridges. During the hot summer months, the court ladies often escaped to these cool places, or rowed about in small boats ornamented with fantastic figureheads.

When regattas were held either on the Irrawaddy, or on the lotus-strewn moat, the Pyi-gyi-mun State Barge was used by the king [75]. This vessel which was pulled by dozens of gilded boats, consisted of two huge canoes clamped together by a platform on which was built cabins with tapering roofs. The figures at the prow depicted celestials and a mythical bird grasping the mane of a dragon. At certain times of the year, the entire court progressed around the moat, each personage aboard a distinctive vessel applicable to his or her rank.

Although the east quarter of Mandalay was reserved for the great monasteries, a few smaller establishments, ornately carved and gilded, together with a pagoda, were also built within and near to the northeastern part of the inner city wall. These oases of tranquillity were for the use of the members of the large royal family and high ranking officials.

The wide streets with their covering of white sand were ideal for pageants, processions and ceremonies. From dawn to dusk, could be seen riders on their caparisoned elephants and horses, and carved palanquins of all shapes and sizes. Each, carrying either an official or a lady, trailed its compliment of brightly costumed retainers holding muskets, long curved swords, emblems of rank and gold umbrellas. A group of drummers and men blowing horns usually accompanied them.

The dress of a court lady consisted of a breast-cloth, a long sleeved jacket open in front, and a richly woven silk skirt which trailed behind her; a shawl was usually draped over the shoulders [99]. A more elaborate costume which was heavily encrusted with sequins and decorated with flame-like appendages stiffened by small canes, was worn for formal occasions when the ladies were officially received by the king and queen in the Hall of the Lily Throne [52]. This was an ornate building situated in the women's quarters, called the Western Palace.

Under an autocratic government it was always considered prudent to be connected to someone with influence; as a result, minor chiefs and the official classes invariably presented their daughters to those in power. Mindon had sixty-three recognized queens and many concubines by whom he fathered over seventy children. Following the death of the king in 1878, some of his offspring were cruelly put to death by of one of his scheming

Shrine of Gaudamas Tooth etc. Mandalay.

The Shrine of Gaudama's Tooth with the Palace Drum Tower on Left. Ahuja.

consorts, and his son Theebaw (r.1878-85) ruled what was left of a once-proud empire. The result was unrest and rebellions throughout the kingdom. In 1885 the British marched into Mandalay and exiled the last of the Konbaung kings to Ratanagiri, in India. The surviving royals, ex-civil servants and their followers were turned out of the walled enclosure and resettled in the main city.

The empty palace had to be made use of and the ornate buildings were promptly taken over by the new military authorities. Many of the grand apartments with their walls of glass mosaic and gilding were whitewashed and used by the army personnel and their Indian clerks. Some of the pavilions in which innumerable court ceremonies had once been held were dismantled. Unfortunately, this vandalism was not stopped until 1901, when Lord Curzon, visiting Mandalay as Viceroy of India, was appalled at the damage and ordered that the palace be restored to its former glory. The fragile old buildings survived until 1945, when they were burnt during the last days of the Japanese Occupation. A replica has now been built by the military regime, and soon a new palace, glinting with what is known locally as 'disco-shway' (plastic gold leaf from Japan), will dominate the Mandalay skyline.

For the tourist of the nineteenth century, visiting the former abode of the King of the Celestial Weapon must have been an unusual experience. Primed by novels and accounts of the last days of Theebaw and his evil Queen Suphayarlat, it must have been exhilarating to inspect at leisure the once forbidden halls and apartments, wherein so much drama, suffering and treachery had been enacted [51].

The British in Upper Burma

Administration, law and order in the former capital was efficiently and quickly established by the British military authorities. During the annexation many of the huge monasteries offered much needed accommodation for the regiments. The resident monks were turned out and unrestrained looting of religious art objects began. Burmese accounts mention British rank and file taking gilded carvings, thinking them to be solid gold, and then smashing them on finding that they were only stone or wood. Some photographs of the period show souvenir hunting soldiers surrounded by native weapons and miscellaneous collections of objets d'art.

Apart from a few incidents, such as attempts by monks and patriotic groups to drive out the British with magic spells, primitive weapons and arson, life continued peacefully for the inhabitants of Mandalay. The local traders made fortunes in providing for the thousands of newly arrived British and Indian troops. Away from the city there was, though, constant unrest as marauding bands of dacoits and members of the former royal army played havoc in the countryside [56, 58].

There was trouble, too, in the Shan States as local rulers called Sawbwa were confronted by the Pax Britannica. In the north-west the Chin-Lushai expedition made headlines in the London papers. Up and down the country royal pretenders appeared; these were either genuine patriots or mercenary opportunists, ruthlessly terrorising simple folk. Invariably it was the people who suffered as the disturbances continued into the early 1900's when the land was finally pacified.

In the early days of the annexation some former ministers were retained for their expertise. These were, though, soon pensioned off to make way for smart young members of the elite ICS (Indian Civil Service) known throughout the Raj as the 'Heaven Born'. Living in the dusty and sweltering heat of Mandalay the pleasant, cool hill station of Maymyo offered a welcome retreat for them. Eventually the administrators left the confines of the city-palace and began to build spacious wooden houses beyond the moat. Here, outwardly at least, life was a gracious round of dinner parties, dances, croquet, tennis and tea parties.

Monasteries and Pagodas

Palace records for 1881 list a staggering 1,257 monasteries in Mandalay, each of which received royal offerings at important moments in the Buddhist calender. These buildings ranged in size from extravagant wood-carved and gilded monasteries to unadorned brick or plain wooden structures. Until the nineteenth century most monasteries were built on a high platform of wood with the often vast empty space beneath used for storage and occassionally to shelter pilgrims or even refugees.

A traditionally built monastery consisted of four separate buildings, sometimes connected by a covered walkway. The most important part was the shrine which was distinguished by a seven-tiered spire [47]. In some monasteries this area also functioned as a library. The three remaining parts were used for ceremonies, sermons, the school room and the monk's living quarters.

In the time of the royal court at Mandalay thousands of yellow-robed monks would enter the walled city each morning to begin their begging rounds. However, this guaranteed supply of sustenance was cut off with the annexation. The year 1886 saw much change in the former capital as the British army took possession of the citadel, effectively isolating the monasteries in the eastern quarter from the main Buddhist population to the west of the walled palace-city. Far from the bustling streets the monks experienced hardship and the slow decline of these once great establishments began. In 1892 a great fire swept through this quarter destroying many of these monasteries, several of which had originally stood in the former capital of Amarapura and had been dismantled and re-erected when King Mindon relocated the capital in 1855. In 1855 Linneaus Tripe photographed certain of these at their original Amarapura site [47]. Thus many splendid creations of the woodcarver's art were lost as well as the magnificent stucco-clad Atu-ma-shi [73, 77]. Miraculously the Shwe-nan-daw Kyaung was spared [68].

The celibate monks led a curious existence. Though bereft of worldly possessions they spent their lives in gilded halls and ate the best food a devotee could afford. Stress-free days were spent poring over manuscripts of the Buddhist law or committing to memory whole texts to be recited before an admiring congregation. When addressing a monk a layperson usually crouched on the floor with hands joined in respect. Many of the the holy brethren were saintly and much venerated. There were, though, a number of young yellow-robed hot-heads known as *yahan-pyo*. They were often feared by the people and generally on the front line of any civic disturbances. Nevertheless, they met their match in the tough Indian policemen who fearing none but Allah did not hesitate to use their truncheons.

Most monasteries, surrounded by shady fruit trees, were oases of peace and tranquility in an otherwise noisy and bustling city. Pilgrims and visitors from afar sought shelter and were made welcome by the monks.

Mandalay, which suffered intense bombardment during the Second World War and as a consequence lost many of its religious buildings, is still a city of pagodas and monasteries. The Raj tourist would have been spoilt for choice, and probably missed out on some of the little known but impressive structures situated away from the main streets. One of these was the Mya-taung Kyaung (Emerald Hill Monastery), the last royal monastery, which was erected between 1884-85 by Suphayarlat. It was built on the profits of the State Lottery, which brought untold misery to many of her subjects. The interior and exterior of the entire structure was carved and lavishly gilded, which led to it being called the Shwe Kyaung (Golden Monastery). Sadly, it did not escape destruction by the Japanese during the Second World War.

Also destroyed was the older and finer Hman Kyaung (The Glass Monastery) built by the queen; its walls and balconies were covered entirely with brilliantly coloured glass mosaic — one of the last masterpieces of this type of craft.

Apart from the palace itself, another attraction in Mandalay was the shrine of the bronze image of Buddha from Arakan, called Mahamuni. It was plundered by the Burmese in 1785, and brought to the then capital of Amarapura. The belief that Buddha himself directed the casting of this image still persists, in spite of archaeological evidence that early Buddhists never made an icon of the Master. The shrine in which it was housed in Arakan had, in the past, been devastated many times, and the image lost; the present icon, vehemently claimed by the Trustees to be the original, probably dates from the fourteenth century. Over the years, the need of the faithful to gain merit by applying gold leaf to the once slim torso of the Mahamuni has given it a bloated appearance.

Other noted religious sites are the Shwe-kyi-myin, built in the twelfth century, which is now home to the gold and be-jewelled images worshipped by the Konbaung kings. The Phayar-Ne (Red Pagoda), to the north of the city, is still rumoured to be haunted by a terrifying *lu-ne* (red man); this has inevitably drawn the curious and no doubt helped to swell the coffers of the shrine. The Shin-bo-mai Pagoda was built in the fifteenth century by the

notorious beauty of the same name, who was queen to five monarchs in succession.

Woodcarvers, weavers, makers of gold-leaf, images and musical instruments together with a host of other artisans, lived in their own quarters in the city. Many can still be seen working in their 'studios' which open on to the street. The huge local bazaar, known as the Zeygyo-daw (royal bazaar) would have drawn the visitor. Within its long covered corridors were shops selling curios, beautifully patterned silk materials and other exotic and bewildering merchandise. It was also the haunt of dashing young men who came from far and wide to stare at some of the fair stall holders. In fact, the Zeygyo-thu (maids of the Zeygyo) were famed for their beauty, grace and quick repartee. Many had Burmese, Chinese, and Indian blood, resulting in stunning good looks which found favour even among the men of the European community.

Beyond Mandalay

Leaving the city and climbing the covered stairways to the top of Mandalay Hill, a wonderful panorama unfolded. To the east the massive blue mountains formed a barrier to the Shan Land. The great sprawling city with its gleaming shrines and turrets lay to the south. Towards the west, the vast Irrawaddy River swirled past the hills of Sagaing. By the river side, a huge dark mass indicated the site of the great Mingun Pagoda, with its gigantic bell which holds the record for being the largest undamaged bell casting in the world.

The megalomaniacking Badon (r.1782-1819) began the near impossible task in the early 1790s of building the immense Mingun Pagoda; work on the unfinished pile dragged on with forced labour until it finally stopped when the king died. Over the years, the whole structure has been broken apart by earthquakes. Hundreds of ceramic reliefs of Buddhist scenes, which were made to be installed around the base, could be seen in a museum nearby; many have now been stolen and smuggled abroad.

From Mandalay, the traveller could either ride to the Shan States, or continue up the Irrawaddy. At Kyauk-hmyaung, a centre for the pottery industry, he would have found the source of the rafts of ceramic jars encountered earlier. Further up at Tagaung, it was possible to visit the shrine of Bo Bo Gyi, a dragon spirit, which was capable of transforming itself into a handsome young man, and who, long ago, seduced a queen of the city. Then

A Burmese Girl. Watts & Skeen.

Burmese Beauties

Possibly the earliest 'studio shots' appeared in C. A. Gordon's *Our Trip to Burmah* (1875). The pictures, which include two Karen and a Burmese lady, are invaluable for students interested in the costumes and textile designs of the nineteenth century. Similar, but unpublished photographs, from a slightly earlier date, also exist in the national collections in Britain.

By the 1890s, photographers such as Beato and Klier were producing large numbers of prints of Burmese ladies. The way in which the models were made to pose hardly varied and was quite unimaginative; the poses consisted either of a seated girl, flanked by potted palms, or standing with a parasol. By about 1910, the photographers at the Ahuja studio were becoming more adventurous. Sets were constructed and the models photographed against this backdrop. One piece of scenery, which contained a tree trunk, was used repeatedly for many years. Fortunately, this has helped the author to identify several anonymously printed portraits as having originated from Ahuja.

Many of the models were simple town girls who enjoyed dressing up in borrowed finery; some professional photographers in Burma still provide a wardrobe section where items can be hired for the occasion. The awkwardness of the maidens is noticeable in their formal poses and wooden expressions. Either seated or standing and holding little posies, they mimic the European beauties of the day. Models invariably placed their hands on the lap, to make sure that the viewer noticed all the beautiful rings on their fingers. In some scenes that supposedly showed a village maid returning from the well, the model appeared bejewelled and in her Sunday best.

Few girls who bought pictures of the glamorous ladies had any secret ambitions of becoming a model — the thought of strange men staring at her picture would have appalled her. And there was, too, the horror of some undesirable character, who having acquired her portrait, would not hesitate to make her his slave by seeking the aid of a powerful black magician.

The author Walter Del Mar warned would-be photographers not to point the camera at a Burmese girl, as she believed that the instrument was capable of allowing the viewer to see her without her clothes 'a liberty which as a modest and moral girl she can't allow.' To know the feeling of ah-shet (shame) separated a well brought up young lady from a brazen hussy.

Paul Edmonds, artist and writer, who was smitten by Burma's doe-eyed ladies, noted that it was difficult for European artists to find models who were prepared to pose in the nude and he quotes an incident in which, out

SW Monsoon Gale Exposing a Leg. Ahuja.

he the tourist would sail past the island at Shwegu, crammed with a 'million' pagodas, where a large fair is held annually. This section of the Irrawaddy, which contains stretches of very deep water, is said to be the haunt of a serpent-like beast called the naga-poke (smelly dragon); the Burmese equivalent of the Loch Ness monster of Scotland. Local fisherfolk claim that their bamboo traps are often raided by the creature.

Beyond Shwegu, the traveller would have entered the land of the Kachins, a fierce warrior race, thence to Bhamo, the ancient gateway to China, through which the mule caravans have trudged back and forth for centuries, and past more stunning mountainous landscapes and cascading streams. In certain areas, the cliffs rise vertically from the banks, and the water becomes so turbulent that navigation is impossible during the rainy season. Here are to be found frightening whirlpools and foaming rapids which feed the great waterway. Finally the traveller would come upon a gentle fertile plain, and the last large town of Myitkyina, or Near the Great River.

of sheer desperation, a young lady of 'doubtful reputation' was finally acquired. When asked to undress she is said to have blushed furiously and fled. Even now in the 1990s, the thought of painting someone in the nude is still claimed to be unthinkable to a Burmese artist.

It would seem that at least one photographer was able to persuade the girl, who appears as 'South West Monsoon Gale', to expose her leg up to an 'indecent' height. Nevertheless, there were sophisticated ladies who become 'professional beauties', and as their fame grew they circulated from studio to studio. These models are identifiable by their poise, and the way they stare confidently at the camera. They stand elegantly, or recline languidly on a chaise longue. There is no doubt that the girls were coached by a European, and made to study the ladies in the post cards produced in the West. It would appear that the poses were artfully calculated with a European customer in mind. Although the models were Oriental, the postures were made to look vaguely Western, which ensured that the picture was acceptable even by the most fastidious of English ladies.

The darling among this new breed of Burmese Beauties was an appropriately named young lady called Sein Chit (Lover of Diamonds), who was also a famous dancer. She had her own theatrical troupe and toured the country with her partner Sein Pu (Petite as a Diamond), and many broken hearts were left in their wake. According to the note, written in English on one post card bearing her picture, she was pronounced 'not bad looking'.

Other equally well known female and male dancers were also used by the studios, as their portraits provided a guaranteed sale among the native population.

It is to be regretted that whenever a studio came across a pretty girl of whatever ethnic background, they invariably dressed her as Burmese lady. As a result, the female national costume of an Arakanese, Manipuri, Mon, or Shan is rarely seen. The picture of the girl, entitled 'Manipur Pride', unfortunately does not show her in her national costume; the bicycle rider with her prominent nose, purporting to be enjoying the advantages of 'Civilization', was probably Anglo-Burmese; a lady reclining uncomfortably on a fur rug and holding a 'whacking great cheroot' has Indian features.

The Raj tourist, although sometimes equipped with a camera, had a large selection of professionally produced images to choose from. Pictures on display in the hotels provided a delightful mixture of chic, innocent and dreamy-eyed ladies in their richly woven skirts. They were certainly contrived to please.

Religious and Secular Festivals

The sound of musical instruments accompanying either a secular or a religious event are heard throughout the year in Burma. All males, assuming they are Buddhists, entered the monastic order temporarily or permanently

A Shin-Byu or Ordination Procession by Elephant.

Sein Chit 'Lover of Diamonds'.

at one time or another. This ceremony occurs during the month of April, just before the rainy season, and soon after the Water Festival celebrations of the New Year.

A boy is eligible to take part in the *shin-byu* (ceremony of initiation) from about the age of ten. Dressed in royal costume, in imitation of Prince Siddhartha who was later to become the Buddha, the boy rides either in a palanquin, or on a horse, or elephant, and is paraded around the town with music and dancing. The little 'princeling' is shaded with gold umbrellas and attended by a retinue of girls carrying offerings. It is a joyous occasion and everyone turns out to murmur blessings as the procession passes by.

Sometimes his little sisters and cousins, dressed like princesses, take a minor part in the celebrations. Fortunately for them, the ritual only consists of having their earlobes pierced; gold or silver needles are used. A wealthy family usually hired a Ponna (Brahmin astrologer) to perform the service. While he recites sacred formulae the orchestra plays loud music to drown out the cries of the apprehensive girls. Guests are fed, and in the evening there are further celebrations in the form of a puppet show, or a variety performance which lasts until dawn.

On arrival at the monastery, the rich costume is taken from the boy, his hair is shaved, and he is clothed in the saffron-coloured robe of the priest. He is then formally accepted into the Order. A dramatic transformation takes place, and the once bright and spirited boy assumes a demeanour of great solemnity. The acolyte remains for a few weeks, attending religious classes, and has to beg for his food in the streets. Many find the discipline to difficult to bear and long to be released back into the indulgent comfort and security of their family.

Burma has been called the 'Land of a Million Pagodas', but it is doubtful whether this is an accurate description, despite the claims by foreign writers and native chronicles. The materials from which pagodas are made can vary from stone and brick to sand. Dry river banks are usually selected for building sand pagodas which are made in cone-shaped tiers, each tier being restrained either by thin broad strips of bamboo, or palm leaves, and decorated with paper flags and tinsel. This, too, is a happy occasion with music and dancing. After prayers are said and the appropriate ceremonies completed, the sand pagodas, now no longer objects of sanctity, are left to the mercy of the elements and are swept away when the river rises.

Each of the larger and more permanent pagodas has a festival day assigned to it. Once the rainy season is over, or when the rice had been

A Burmese Orchestra and Actors Performing. Watts & Skeen.

harvested, there is a round of pagoda fairs. This is a busy period for itinerant vendors who travel to each venue in rotation. In Burma, religion, business and pleasure go casually hand in hand. Having performed one's duty of praying at the shrine one goes out to spend or make a little money and enjoy the entertainments provided by the trustees.

Pageants are held either on feast days or during pagoda festivals. Depending on the wealth of the community these can be organized on a grand scale with decorated floats, or long caravans of bullock-carts bearing dancing girls, or costumed youngsters. Stops are made along the way when scenes from the Birth Stories of the Buddha are acted out.

Periodically, a famous relic or an image would be taken on a tour by its guardians and if the journey involved travelling down the Irrawaddy, the steamer bearing the sacred object would be gaily decorated and accompanied by an orchestra. The vessel would stop frequently along the route, so that the river-side villagers would have the opportunity to worship and make offerings. On its departure, the more mobile would run along the river bank until the boundary pillars of their village were reached. Then, the neighbouing villagers would take over. Many would travel in from afar to worship from the bank.

In town, the relic would be either carried on a palanquin by saintly men, or borne on a float in the shape of a sacred white elephant. Youths and maidens dressed as heavenly beings were in attendance. Depending on the importance of the holy object varying forms of piety could be witnessed. Ladies would offer their jewellery, while others crouched on the earth and spread their long hair (a source of feminine pride) so that the men or vehicle carrying the relic would pass over it. Imbued with genuine piety many swooned in the presence of the sacred object.

Another fairly common sight on the outskirts of towns and villages would have been the cremation ceremony of a monk. Whenever a senior and wise member of the holy order passed away, the local people pooled together their resources to give him an impressive funeral. Flat open ground was selected for the event. Within days the area would be transformed into a huge fair and bazaar, with gigantic bamboo and paper structures of the most exotic shapes [67]. The ceremony of lying in state could last for days. Every kind of entertainment was provided for those who wished to pay their respects. It was not a time of sadness but for celebration, as it was believed that the soul of the monk which had been released from his earthly bondage was now about to ascend to a higher and nobler dimension.

While awaiting cremation in the Hall of the Dead, the corpse was laid in a coffin and covered in honey. It was then placed in a gleaming sarcophagus suspended on ropes. Professional female mourners in court dress then swung it gently, singing ancient dirges, and extolling the virtues of the deceased. On the last day the coffin was removed from the hall and placed in one of the tall buildings, around which had been heaped firewood [91]. At the appointed time huge rockets were fired at the base, until finally the elaborate edifice caught fire. Needless to say, honey which appeared in the local bazaar after a monk's cremation was usually viewed with suspicion.

Funerals for lesser mortals could also be impressive. Here, too, an orchestra or a puppet troupe would be hired to entertain friends who had come to support the bereaved family. The plays performed were suitably sombre. Until the end of the nineteenth century, funeral processions were usually proceeded by drummers executing slow stately movements. Seven days after the burial, a group of monks and mourners were fed.

But the Burmese are not a melancholy race and are aware from a young age that death is inevitable for all living things. Soon, the sound of distant booming drums and shrill clarinets, would invariably draw them either to a marionette show or a play.

The Burmese Theatre

Evidence for the popularity of the dance in Burma can be seen in terracotta plaques from as early as the seventh-century AD. Chinese sources, from the T'ang dynasty (618-907), have also left accounts of cultural missions made up of a mixed group of Pyu and Mon entertainers, who appeared at their capital Ch'ang-an in the ninth century. The wall paintings of the Pagan period (1044-1287) testify that music and dance were enjoyed by the Burmese people. Judging from the postures of the performers, however, the movements appear to have been influenced by Indian forms of dancing. Native chronicles of a later date mention the employment of dancers at court, and that the ceremonial duties of the sovereign were accompanied by music.

Under a monarch with imperialistic urges, the Burmese raided surrounding countries for loot and skilled artisans. The three momentous occasions when this occurred on a grand scale were in 1057, 1567 and 1767, when among the captives brought back to the capitals of Pagan, Pegu, and Ava were dancers and musicians. These unfortunate people were pressed into service, and on each occasion enhanced and raised the standard of entertainment at court. The invasion of Ayutthaya in 1767 is beleived to have benefited the the state of the arts in Burma the most. Thai music and dance, known as *yodaya*, became extremely popular, and was the highlight of a performance in the Burmese palace. The plays requested most avidly were of Thai origin.

King Theebaw and Suphayarlat were keen patrons of the performing arts, and were entertained both by the court troupe and by itinerant theatrical companies. During the first half of the 1880s, shows were held either on a grand scale in the theatre or were informal affairs, with the royal pair watching from a rustic summer house. It was a centuries-old tradition that the dancers performed on ground level; only a puppet troupe was allowed the use of a stage.

During the dry cool months between October and March, theatrical performances were also held in the compounds of princes, and high dignitaries. Some of the inhabitants of Mandalay compared the walled city to paradise, for melodious music issued from various orchestras through the night. But for those who fell foul of the dreaded Suphayarlat and awaited her pleasure in the torture chambers, the palace city must have been the very pit of hell.

The Thai form of dancing retained its superiority over native forms until the demise of the monarchy in 1885, when with the annexation by the British of the entire country, new music and dance styles were invented, and the slow movements of the Thai dancers suddenly became old fashioned.

It must be said that professional dancers did not hold the exclusive right to entertain. Dancing comes naturally even to the smallest Burmese child. At state functions or receptions it was usually the children or young ladies from the upper classes who performed for the assembled dignitaries [63]. Although members of the dancing profession were considered to belong to a lower order, it was nevertheless quite acceptable to have young girls of good families performing in public [92]. Women in Burma have always enjoyed a considerable amount of freedom and have never had to live in seclusion.

Until about 1900, the majority of theatrical troupes performed on the ground; in a style called *myai-waing* (earth circle). The show was a simple affair without scenery, and the performance took place in front of an orchestra. A leafy branch symbolized the forest, and a property chest could become either a boat or a flying chariot. Masks which were to be used during a play were usually hung on a bamboo pole above the orchestra, and taken down as the occasion demanded. The arena was lit by oil lamps. It was a very public affair, with the players changing in to their costume in full view of the audience. Apart from the village girls shyly watching the actresses making up, the actors were ignored by the crowd when not performing. But once the performance commenced and the actors took their place the area was transformed by the spectator's imagination. The voices of the characters, and the appropriate music, indicated to the audience a particular setting. When foreign shows started to appear in Rangoon and Mandalay, the Burmese theatrical profession was quick to adapt and a stage was adopted. For many, the new style of theatre with scenery, modern lighting and curtains must have been a novel sight. Plays were either based on Buddhist stories, or the increasingly popular modern pieces which were produced at a prodigious rate by young scriptwriters from Lower Burma.

Where once performances were free, many troupes now began to charge an entrance fee. Shows were held in halls, corrugated iron sheds, or temporary buildings of bamboo matting. However, there were still small companies which performed in the traditional way. These usually consisted of two female dancers, a clown, and a few musicians. They either presented excerpts from plays, with one of the ladies assuming the role of the leading male character, or entertained with the latest songs and dances. Among such

Burmese Racing Canoes. Ahuja .

troupes a few female dancers acquired fame in their impersonations of a Mintha (male lead). Conversely, some young men took to appearing as a Minthamee (leading lady). The quality of acting and dancing presented by the latter was often considered to be superior to that of a female.

The leading exponent in this field was a delicate young man called Aung Bala or Victorious Strength, who was partnered by a succession of well known male dancers of the day [78]. Simple young peasants were encouraged to believe by their mischievous friends in town that the 'leading lady' was indeed a sweet young maid, and urged them to send love letters; a number were said to have been devastated when the truth was revealed.

By 1900, the leading male dancer was one Po Sein or Master Diamond [78]. From being a relatively unknown performer, he found fame after becoming the partner of the celebrated female impersonator, Aung Bala. Po Sein sensed the need for change, choreographed new dance styles, and commissioned bold love songs which some of the older people among the audience found objectionable; the young, however, were impressed. Po Sein is said to have won over the traditionalists by the sheer force of his personality. He became immensely popular, and the ladies showered him with presents. The lead dancers from other theatrical companies soon began to imitate his style.

Some photographs, from about 1905, show dancers dressed in inappropriate

A Woodcarver, Rangoon.

A theatrical performance usually commenced at about 9 pm and lasted until dawn. Traditionally, only one play was presented, but from about 1900 the presentation became more ambitious with chorus girls and short sketches. The first half of the evening consisted mainly of singing and dancing. It was said that the components necessary for a successful company were witty clowns, actors, and actresses, who sang and danced well, and a good orchestra. With the increase in the number of theatrical troupes many other attendant professions also began to reap the benefits; costumiers, artists, the makers of musical instruments, as well as carters, and boatmen to provide transport.

In rural areas, a caravan of carts or string of vessels carrying entertainers arrived at their destination with music playing loudly, attracting hoards of barking dogs and wide-eyed children.

costumes. This was invariably done at the request of the European photographer who was totally ignorant of the traditions of the Burmese theatre. An example of this was entitled 'A Burmese Princess' (the model was a dancer called Ma Aye Sein) dressed in the ornate costume of the male lead from the Ramayana — a classical drama. The company had no hesitation in printing another card which showed her in the same robe, but in the act of performing the energetic *ozi* (drum) dance usually performed by strapping country lads; the incongruity of the costume was to cause amazement among older Burmese [78]. These pictures, which were circulated all over the country, were probably responsible for the deterioration in the standard of dress once maintained by theatrical troupes.

Until well into this century a large number of Burmese males wore their long hair in a topknot, which was usually hidden under a turban. The actor or dancer, on the other hand, simply wound an ornate scarf around the head which left the coiled hair exposed. Po Sein and his contemporaries soon began decorating the top knot with flowers and hairpins, starting a trend which continues today. This form of ornamentation, together with the richly embroidered flowing *pasoe* (sarong), tight fitting sequinned jacket, jewellery, and almost female style of makeup, still confuses Western 'experts' on Burmese culture, who are often at a loss to identify the sex of a dancer, or member of the cast.

Burmese Life

Boat builders and cartwrights have prospered in Burma since its earliest history. Evidence of their craft has been immortalized in works of art from as early as the eleventh century. As in most countries the economy of the kingdom was based on the fruits of agriculture and trade. Before colonization by the British the rural population was self sufficient, and on market days forays were made to the nearest towns or larger villages to acquire what was unobtainable locally.

Country carts were sturdy and made to withstand the rough tracks which often became waterlogged during the rains [96]. Old paintings show carts with wheels which have been sawn from huge teak trunks.

In Mandalay, cartwrights lavished their skill on their creations and commissioned decorative rails from woodcarvers. Side panels, terminating in pieces curving upwards, were often wrought with floral patterns, the intricacy of craftsmanship in keeping with the station one occupied in life [95]. The shaft between the bullocks was usually in the shape of either a bird, dancer, or a dragon. Shade was provided by a curved roof of finely woven bamboo. Carts for the official classes often had additional cloth covers of applique work. Trappings for the bullocks consisted of collars and lengths of either leather or thick cloth cut in to flame shapes, and decorated with sequins, small mirrors, and tiny brass bells. Other accessories were rugs for the cart (spread over a layer of hay) and thick tasselled braid, which hung from the flanks of the beasts. These were made by craftsmen who specialized in horse,

Tattooing a Burmese Boy. Watts & Skeen.

Burmese Potter.
American Baptist
Missionary Press.

elephant, and cart furnishings.

According to photographs obtained from some of the photographs, variations in cart design existed among the Burmese, Arakanese, Mon, and the Karen. Unfortunately, the once beautifully made and regionally identifiable carts are no more.

Travellers on the waterways depended on the boat builders of Pakokku, who were renowned for their splendid, distinctively Burmese boats and barges. Before the arrival of the European-owned paddle steamers in the mid nineteenth century, many of these fine vessels carried passengers and cargo. Because of the sumptuary laws, large sailing boats built before 1885 were rarely decorated, but with the fall of the dynasty vessels with elaborately decorated sterns began to appear [74].

The most popular sport of the towns and villages close to water was boat racing. Huge teak logs were shaped into long canoes either by professionals or enthusiasts. The rowers, about sixteen men to each canoe, were responsible for its maintenance. After a day in the fields, the men would gather at a rendezvous where 'boat songs' were learnt, the latest gossip concerning their rivals exchanged and strategies discussed, along with the consumption of much tea and candies made from toddy palm and sugarcane. Talk was of the defensive systems employed during the days of the monarchy when men were taught the thirty-seven ways of employing a paddle; the strokes were honed and improved by generations of rowers of war canoes. One of these involved the use of the oars to produce a screen of water to confuse the enemy.

On the day of the boat race the excitement among the onlookers was intense. It was a time, too, when those taking part could show off their physique before the admiring glances of the village beauties. With sarongs tucked up defiantly between their tattooed legs, and long hair knotted at a rakish angle, the men would posture full of bravado on the riverbank.

A youth did not consider himself a proper man until he had had his thighs tattooed. The designs, produced by a travelling tattooist, varied from the purely ornamental, to diagrams of magical charms which were believed to give protection from occult dangers, induce bravery in war, or as an aid to sexual potency. The tradition of tattooing was so ingrained that even in paintings and carvings of men the appropriate marks were faithfully depicted with.

Secular habitation, like monasteries, was usually built of wood and bamboo. Because of the danger from earthquakes this may have been advisable, but it was also a fire hazard. The chronicles often recorded conflagrations at the capital which destroyed everything in their path, sparing neither the grand palaces, gilded monasteries, nor the humblest of huts. As a result substantial examples in wood of more than 200 years old are rare.

The Burmese delight in carving. Once the crops had been gathered a farmer often turned his hand to ornamenting the handle of his water cup, carving a family altar, or decorations for his cart and his wife's loom.

At court the guild of wood carvers were divided into two ranks; those who produced furniture and architectural pieces were considered junior to those who carved statuary for use within the palace or royal monasteries. Until the seventeenth century it was forbidden for a commoner to build a monastery embellished with carvings; this was the privilege of the royal family and high dignitaries. This restriction had effectively been removed by the second half of the nineteenth century, as can be seen in the photographs taken by Captain Tripe and others.

Art forms can only flourish during times of peace and prosperity. For the wood carver and the architect the periods between 1860 and 1925 were probably the most lucrative. In Rangoon newly rich merchants vied with each other to build ornate shrines and halls on the platform of the Shwe Dagon Pagoda. Not to be outdone, their counterparts in rural areas sent for the most famous of craftsmen from Mandalay to decorate their local stupas. Some of the oldest examples of the woodcarver's art can still be seen at the ancient city of Pagan; but civil wars and fire have destroyed many.

Some sculptors worked for European dealers settled in the country, who might have had establishments selling curios. Examples from such sources are now considered ugly by purists, as the carvers had to follow the dictates of a foreigner attempting to make native work acceptable to western tastes. Desks, screens, chairs, and numerous other European pieces of furniture were laboriously carved with designs from Burmese mythology that were often inappropriate.

Other wood carvers worked from 'studios' in the long corridors leading to well known pagodas. They maintained the true Burmese style in the shape of Buddhist and animist icons, manuscript chests, thrones for images and ornate seats for ecclesiastical dignitaries. With the increase in foreign tourists, some began producing exquisitely carved and painted statuettes of the numerous tribal groups in the country.

Household items, such as plates, bowls, and storage boxes were originally made by specialist workers in wood. The commonest boxes had a base of woven bamboo which was coated and decorated with black or red lacquer. But soon foreign imports, usually of tin and porcelain, began replacing the native products in the larger towns and cities.

Another craft, associated with woodcarving and lacquer, was *hman-si-shway-cha*. It involved the use of tiny pieces of shaped multi-coloured glass, which are embedded in a malleable mixture of ash and lacquer; when dry the object would be gilded.

The production of gold leaf was to serve the insatiable appetites of Buddhist seekers of merit. Originally, large quantities were imported from China via Yunnan. Goldleaf makers required strength and stamina. The process involved placing tiny nuggets between squares of leather, and pounding the pack until the desired thinness was achieved. Pagodas and images, of which there are many thousands, are continually gilded by the pious. Even today vast amounts are still being spent on gold leaf.

A Burmese crowd in festive mood enjoy dressing in their finery. While the ruling classes were able to afford foreign material, until the second half of the nineteenth century many rural people wove their own cloth. Very little is known about the early history of the Burmese loom, but with the introduction of skilled weavers from subjugated kingdoms, the art improved dramatically. Although cotton is still grown in the country, at the time, raw silk was imported from China.

The second half of the nineteenth century saw the quality of design of the *htamein* (ladies' skirt), and the *pasoe* (mens' sarong) reach its peak. These lengths of cloth, required as many as 100 shuttles to weave, came in various patterns and each strip was known by a poetic title. The weaver either duplicated one pattern down the entire length or else wove a mixture of designs.

Each design was composed of flowers, waves, birds, and a pattern based on lightning flashes. A weaver could thus produce a multitude of variations. The vibrant colours were skilfully tempered with subtler hues. These textiles were only worn on high days and holidays, and were stored away carefully.

Although umbrellas are featured in the wall paintings of the eleventh century, they are usually seen in association either with religion or royalty; one of the many titles used by a Burmese king is 'Lord of All Umbrella Bearing Chiefs'. Senior clergy, members of the royal family, and the official classes, were allocated gilded umbrellas according to their rank, but the man in the street was not allowed the use of even a plain one. For him, the only form of protection from the tropical sun was a broad-brimmed bamboo hat; these were produced in huge quantities.

From about 1910, umbrellas for ladies began appearing with decorations painted in water-soluble colours. The patterns were originally of flowers, and the umbrella could obviously be used only as a sunshade. From simple designs, the umbrella makers later progressed to scenes from plays, and the Birth Stories of the Buddha, though these were intended only for the tourist trade. Bassein, in Lower Burma, is still famous for its ornamented silk umbrellas.

Some makers specialized in umbrellas of white linen or satin, which they decorated with imitation jewels, gold, and silver foil. These were of a bulbous shape and were intended to shade the corpse of an eminent monk, to be carried during a religious procession, or to be placed behind an image of the Buddha.

The number of these images commissioned since earliest times is prodigious. Although six postures are known, only one known as the *bhumisparsa* (earth- touching) was really popular. The images come in all sizes, from the minute to the huge monoliths seen around Mandalay and Pagan. They were made of either brick, stone, metal, lacquer or wood. The making of images was also practised by the Mon, Arakanese, and other ethnic groups in the Shan States. Although like the Burmese they, too, favoured the Buddha in the earth-touching posture, facial and ornamental differences are recognizable. Towards the end of the nineteenth century it became the trend to commission images made by the Burmese craftsmen of Mandalay and Sagaing, which caused hardship for those in other parts of the country.

Workers in metal either specialized in casting images, or produced more readily saleable objects such as household utensils, agricultural implements, weapons, gongs, and cone-shaped fretwork finials for pagodas. Some made architectural embellishments, which were cut out of sheets of tin, and were shaped to look like wood carving. The surface was then covered in lacquer, glass mosaic and gilding and could hardly be distinguished from decorated wood.

The production of lacquerware is traditionally believed to have been introduced to Pagan, in 1057 by Mon captives. It is still made in large quantities and appears to be the preserve of the Burmans from the central and arid part of the country.

Next to lacquerware, the art of the potter has to be numbered among the oldest crafts in the country. One of the legacies of the ancient Pyu is the enormous number of beautifully decorated burial urns which have been excavated. The Martaban jars which were once exported all over the Orient by the Mon are still being made by their descendants, whose forefathers had been taken captive in the eighteenth century by the Burmese and relocated to Kyauk-hmyaung, in Upper Burma.

Storage vessels and drinking water pots, continue to be produced in various parts of Burma, especially at the old Mon village of Twante, near Rangoon. Regional styles are still distinguishable.

With its lush vegetation, Burma abounds in snakes of various kinds, and the thickly wooded slopes of Mount Popa, in particular, offer ideal conditions for these reptiles. During the dry season snake charmers are often seen performing in the streets. The Burmese loathe snakes and usually kill them on sight, but a performance always draws a large fascinated crowd.

Before a snake could be caught permission had to be sought from the local spirits. The snake charmer had to take an oath stating that the reptile would be released within a certain period; failure to do so was said to be fatal. Some had the fangs removed, others left them intact, believing in the power of the amulets they wore. Unlike the snake charmers of India the performer does not blow a flute but dances before the snake, which is reputedly forcefed on sticky rice to make it lethargic.

Snake charmers traded on their supposed power to subdue the most poisonous of snakes, and sold charms or designed tattoos with magical diagrams. If a protected person succumbed to a snake bite, it was believed that he had been guilty of doing something to anger the spirits. Doubts were rarely cast on the qualifications of the snake charmer. This form of protection was popular with rural people who had to face the daily hazard of encountering poisonous reptiles.

Ethnic Groups

Foreign visitors who were interested in the more remote ethnic groups of the country but who were unable to attempt the journey into the interior, sometimes had the pleasure of seeing their 'quarry' in the cosmopolitan setting of Rangoon. The colourful little parties undertaking arduous pilgrimages from their remote tribal villages were mainly of the Buddhist faith, but some were Christians who nevertheless came to gape in wonder at the gilded shrines of the capital. During the cool season these pilgrims, dressed in their distinctive costumes, could be glimpsed on the platform of the Shwe Dagon. Here, they wandered wide-eyed and incredulous at the dazzling display of gold. Later, they would timidly shuffle along the pavements of the main streets, overwhelmed by the sights and sounds of the modern city.

In the late nineteenth century there were over sixty recorded ethnic groups. This number has dwindled because of intermarriage and post-war governments' policies of integration. Many now dress in the Burmese style, and are gradually loosing their ethnic identity.

The Buddhist Shan (Tai) live on the borders of China, Laos and Thailand, in one of the most beautiful and mountainous parts of the country. For centuries, the land was fragmented into small states each ruled by a Sawbwa (Prince). In the sixteenth century the Shan overran Upper Burma and ousted the Burmese dynasty. But they were incapable of consolidating their power, and wasted their energy fighting among themselves. They were soon brought under the Burmese yoke, and until

1885 were governed as tributary chiefs.

Ceremonies at the Shan courts were based on those of their Burmese overlord, who saw to it that they observed the sumptuary laws in use at the Burmese capital. The chiefs were given the title of Kings of the Sunset, to impress upon them that they occupied an inferior position in the hierarchy. With the annexation of Upper Burma by the British the yoke was lifted, and they were allowed to rule their own states. The princes held court in their palaces until the 1950s, when they were removed from power by the Burmese government.

Shan males from the rural areas were heavily tattooed. Each man sported a distinctive pattern of animals, spirits, and elaborately written spells. Their braves excelled in the use of the long sword and lance, and were valued at the Burmese court [103]. Shan craftsmen are still noted for their superbly made lacquerware, swords, daggers, and their skill in carving ivory. Their culture, costume, language and script is quite distinct from the rest of Burma.

The Chin, Kachin and the Karen did not possess a written language and as a result the background history for these groups can only be found in oral traditions, and folk tales. Although the art of tattooing was known among the Chin, it was only used as a form of defence by young women. This consisted of complicated tattoo patterns which covered the entire face, and were designed to deter marauding Burmese soldiers. This practice ceased towards the end of the nineteenth century, as their homeland gradually came under more organized British administration.

There were once many clans among the Chin. Variations could be seen in the way the men dressed their long hair; those from the north tied theirs in a knot at the nape of the neck, while the southerners sported a top-knot. Like the Kachin, the men were noted for their bravery. Ceremonial dress consisted of woven blankets, with decorations which identified the particular clan and social position of its owner.

The Kachin claim that they once lived in Tibet, and that their original name of Sin-po was the term used to describe a cannibal in the Tibetan tongue. Centuries ago when the ancestors of these hardy men descended from their snowy plateau in to northern Burma, they ousted the original inhabitants, such as the Chin, Palaung, and the Shan; many were killed in raids and their cremated remains buried under large mounds which can still be seen. Until the annexation the Kachin continually harried the Burmese and the Shan [104].

Group of Wa Tribesmen. Group of Was (Head Hunters)

The Karen were originally animists, but during the nineteenth century entire villages were converted to Christianity. Many took to the new religion to seek the protection of the British authorities, as they had suffered harsh oppression for centuries under the Burmese. Karen clans, too, were recognizable by the patterns woven on their clothes. Those living in towns, and considered 'civilized' by the Burmese, usually wore the *longyi* (sarong) or the *htamein*. Perhaps because of their timidity, due to years of oppression, Karen levies were never employed at the Burmese court. What little has survived of their craft is to be found mainly in woven materials and basketry.

Among the many tribal groups in the country, the Padaung are still the most exotic, and featured prominently as living exhibits at state celebrations organised by the British. The 'giraffe-necked women' made use of coiled lengths of brass to protect their necks, it was claimed, from the bite of a tiger. The Padaung ladies, however, discount this explanation and insist that the rings enhanced their beauty.

Other tribes such as the Wa and Naga inhabited wild peaks and terrified the surrounding ethnic groups. For them head-hunting raids and chilling human sacrifice rituals were a way of life until the early years of this century. By contrast, the peace-loving Taungthu, and the musically minded Kaw, the aristocratic Khun, and the shy Lahu presented the gentler side of these dwellers of the hills.

Having travelled through this ever changing land-scape, and observed the 'children of the Empire', the exhausted traveller would have been relieved to return to the comforts of Rangoon, with its paved streets and imposing buildings.

Many of the monuments depicted in this book no longer exist, and the smiling Burmese beauties have grown old and died. But trapped within these sepia coloured photographs and tinted little scraps of board, each subject remains fixed, immutable, at the precise moment the shutter clicked somewhere in colonial Burma.

The Sawbwa of Yawnghwe. P. Klier.

Photographers and Post Card Publishers

Air Survey Co. Ltd.
American Baptist Mission Press, Rangoon.
Verlag v. Albert Aust, Hamburg.
Banzai Brothers & Co. (Japan), Mandalay and Rangoon.
Felice A. Beato, Mandalay and Rangoon.
Bourne and Shepherd, Calcutta.
Burma Railways, Rangoon.
Burma Rifles, Rangoon.
Sir Joseph Causton & Sons Ltd., London.
Louis Daguerre.
Desai and Friends, Maymyo.
M. Fuji & Co., Rangoon.
P.G. Hunt, Deansgate, Manchester, England.
Illustrated Missionary News, Rangoon.
Imperial Institute, Rangoon.
J. Jackson, Rangoon.
"Printed in Japan."
"K" Ltd.
Peter Klier, Rangoon.
Kundan-Dass and Co., Rangoon.
Lekhraj & Sons, Rangoon.
John MacCosh.
Godfrey Phillips Ltd.
The Phototype Co., Bombay.
R. Raphael, Bassein.
Rowe & Co. Ltd., Rangoon.
Royal Hotel, Rangoon.
S.P.G. Missionary Postcards, Rangoon.
Myles Standish & Co., Rangoon.
S.N. Samuels, Mandalay.
Solar Film Series, London.
H. Stiller & Co., Ltd.
Tripe, Captain Linneaus.
Raphael Tuck & Sons "Oilette," London, England.
Wagstaff & Co., Photographic Artists, Rangoon.
Watts and Skeen Series (The Hanthawaddy Press), Rangoon.
Weltreise "Verlag Compagnie Comet" (Fr.Th. & Co.) Dresden.
Wesleyan Methodist Mission Society, Mandalay.
Yadanabon Bawga Yaza Co., Mandalay.
Yamada & Co., Mandalay and Rangoon.

Bibliography

Bird, George, W. *Wanderings in Burma*, Simpkin, Marshall, Hamilton, Kent and Co., London, 1897.
Grant Brown, R. *Burma As I Saw It (1889-1917)*, Methuen and Co, London, 1926.
Bruce, George. *The Burma Wars, 1824-1886*, Hart-Davis, MacGibbon, London, 1973.
Collis, Maurice. *Lords of the Sunset (A Tour in the Shan States)*, Faber and Faber, London, 1938.
Cuming, E.D. *In the Shadow of the Pagoda*, W.H. Allen and Co., London, 1897.
Del Mar, Walter. *The Romantic East: Burma, Assam and Kashmir*, A. & C. Black, London, 1906.
Edmonds, Paul. *Peacocks and Pagodas*, George Routeledge and Sons, Ltd., London, 1924.
Ferrars, Max and Bertha. *Burma*, Sampson Low, Marston and Co, London, 1900.
Gordon, C.A. *Our Trip to Burmah*, Bailliere, Trindall and Cox, London, 1875.
Fielding Hall, H. *The Soul of a People*, Macmillan and Co, London 1911.
    A People at School, Macmillan and Co., London, 1913.
Hart, Mrs Ernest. *Picturesque Burma, Past and Present*, J.M. Dent and Co., London, 1897.
McCrae, Alister. *Scots in Burma: Golden Times in a Golden Land*, Kiscadale Publications, Edinburgh, 1990.
Mitton, G.E., *A Bachelor Girl in Burma*, A. & C. Black, London 1907.
Scott O'Connor, V.C. *The Silken East: A Record of Life and Travel in Burma*, Kiscadale Publications, Gartmore, 1993.
    Mandalay and Other Cities of the Past in Burma, Hutchinson and Co, London, 1907.
Talbot Kelly, R. *Burma Painted and Described*, A. & C. Black, London, 1905.
Thorp, Ellen. *Quiet Skies on Salween*, Jonathan Cape, London, 1945.
Trench Gascoigne, Gwendolen. *Among Pagodas and Fair Ladies*, A.D. Innes and Co., London, 1896.
Thirkell White, Sir Herbert. *A Civil Servant in Burma*, Edward Arnold, London, 1913.
Wills, A.W. *Sunny Days in Burma*, Printed privately at the Midland Counties Herald Press, London 1905.

Sule Pagoda and Fytch Square, Rangoon. On the right of the pagoda is the Town Hall. In the distance can be seen the Shwe Dagon Pagoda. Until the 1860s old Rangoon was swampy and tidal creeks flooded the area around the Sule Pagoda at high tide. Klier.

33 *Rangoon* - ဆူးလေ(ကျိုက်အသုတ်)စေတီနှင့်မြို့တော်ခမ်းမရှုခင်း

Merchant Street, Rangoon. In A *History of Rangoon*, a similar engraving, probably based on the photograph, has a caption 'Merchant Street, 1869'. By 1885 Rangoon was a well-developed city with many splendid brick public buildings. The quality of the photograph and the scene indicate that it was taken sometime during the late 1860s. On the far right is the Sule Pagoda.

၁၈၆၉ခုနှစ်တွင်ရိုက်ကူးထားသောရန်ကုန်မြို့ကုန်သည်လမ်း – *Rangoon 34*

The Mosque in Mogul Street, Rangoon. Circa 1890.

South Entrance to the Shwe Dagon Pagoda, Rangoon. Taken sometime before
1887. The old entrance with guardian demons, constructed by King Tharawaddy
(r.1837-46) can still be seen. On each side of the road are pilgrim's rest houses.
Carriages in Rangoon were owned by Indians.

၁၈၈၇ခုနှစ်မတိုင်မီရိုက်ကူးထားသောရွှေတိဂုံစေတီတော်တောင်ဖက်မုတ် – *The Shwe Dagon 36*

ENTRANCE OF SHWE DAGONE PAGODA 503,
KLIER RANGOON

COPYRIGHT

South Entrance to the Shwe Dagon Pagoda, Rangoon. The two large *chinthe lions* were built in 1887. In that year, the remainder of the original brick entrance was ornamented with scenes of fabulous beasts and spirits. Klier.

37 The Shwe Dagon - ၁၈၈၇ခုနှစ်တွင်ပွဲစားတစ်ဦးလှူဒါန်းခဲ့သောရွှေတိဂုံတောင်ဖက်မုခ်မုခ်မှန်သေ့ကြီးများ

The Shwe Dagon Pagoda. c. 1860s. A large number of small shrines were built on the lower platforms in the early 1880s by the new wealthy classes of British Burma. Each corner of the huge pagoda is guarded by a sphinx-like creature with two bodies, attended on each side by three lions.

Entrance to the Main Platform, Shwe Dagon Pagoda. The inscription says that the pavilion was built in 1888. Wood carvings between the pillars depict a scene from the history of the pagoda. On the right the Mon brothers Phussa and Bhandika are shown arriving in carts, guided by Sule nat towards the Buddha on the left. In the centre is a scene from the Vidhura *Jataka:* the minister Vidhura is threatened by a demon.

The Pavilion of the Great Bell, Shwe Dagon Pagoda. The pagoda in the background is the Naung-daw-gyi, and is believed to be older than the Shwe Dagon. On the right in front of the tall mast, can be seen a model of the previous finial of the Shwe Dagon pagoda. Klier.

RANGOON RIVER, THE MOULMEIN STEAMER ARRIVING

The Moulmein Steamer Arriving at Rangoon.

On the River. Above: steamers of the Irrawaddy Flotilla Company are moored against the river bank. Below left: an elephant used to transport logs to the river. Below right: Burmese cargo boats used to transport paddy and other produce to the Rangoon docks for export.

Monasteries and Pagodas at Moulmein. The architecture is quite distinct from
that of Upper Burma. Probably photographed c.1890 by Klier who often included his
Indian servant in the picture.

LARGE IMAGE AT PEGU

The Shwe-thar-ly-aung, Pegu. Traditionally believed to have been built by King Migadipa in 944 AD. It was restored by Ramadhipatiraja (r.1472-1492) but later 'lost' and recovered from the jungle in the 1880s by an Indian contractor called Nalabi, who proceeded to dig up the bricks. He was promptly stopped by Buddhists, who restored the image. Unfortunately, it has now lost its original Mon features.

Novices Returning to their Monastery with their Alms Bowls.

A Sayadaw and Disciple. This post card was reproduced from a studio portrait. Monks were not allowed to handle money so were often accompanied by a lay disciple who carried the purse. Klier.

Hpongyi's Before their Monastery. The pillars have been embellished with magnificent carvings of the *naga* or sea serpent.

The Elephant Trap. Probably one of the last elephant roundups to be staged at the elephant trap which was built by King Tharawaddy (r.1837-46) at Amarapura. The wild elephants were decoyed into the stockade and teased into exhaustion by the spectators. Part of the central enclosure on the left contained a shrine to U Deinna, a spirit associated with elephants; it was said to soothe the troubled beasts with the sound of its harp. Beato.

The No Monastery at Amarapura. 1855, Tripe.

The Taung-min-gyi Image at Amarapura. 1855, Tripe.

၁၈၅၅ခုနှစ်တွင်ရိုက်ကူးထားသောတောင်မင်းကီးရုပ်ပွါးတော်ကြီးဘ

Women Bathing in the Irrawaddy. Traditionally Burmese people take a minimum of two baths a day. The Shwe-kyet-yet Pagoda can be seen in the background.

West Gate to the Palace City at Mandalay. This was known as the 'Gate of Ill Omen', and was used for condemned prisoners, funeral processions, or when people were sent into exile. To the east are the Shan Hills. Beato.

The *Myei-nan* or Main Audience Hall, Mandalay Palace. This huge structure, known as the 'Centre of the Universe', contained the principal *The-ha-thana* (Lion Throne), a replica of which was also used in the *Hlutdaw* or Privy Council. Behind the seven-roofed spire can be seen the roof of the Zay-ta-wun-saung which housed the *Hantha-thana* (Hamsa Throne) and the royal archives. Bamboo partitions were erected around the hall which was originally open by the Engineering Department after the fall of Mandalay. Beato.

A Gateway to the Inner Palace. Klier.

Below: King Theebaw and Queen Suphayarlat. This is a collage, the royal couple are shown framed by carvings which depict scenes from the legend of the Shwe Dagon Pagoda.

The *The-ha-thana* or Lion Throne. It was used in the *Myei-nan*. In each of the little niches in the middle section of the throne was placed a small figure of a lion. On the floor below was a row composed of alternating gilded figures of a male child, with his hands raised in salutation, and a lion. There were eight of the former and nine of the latter. There were also four *camari*, a stylized representation of the Tibetan yak, and a pair of larger lions. Beato.

51 Mandalay – နန်းတွင်းသို့အဝင်။ သီပေါဘုရင်နှင့်မြတောင်စုဘုရား:လတ်။   မြန်းပြသာဒ်တော်ကြီးအတွင်းမှသီဟာသနပလ္လင်တော်ကြီး

A Burmese Princess. A princess in court dress is photographed standing on one of the brick terraces of the palace at Mandalay. The elaborate court costumes of velvet, satin and silk were encrusted with imitation jewels and sequins, the flame-like front and tail pieces were held up by small pieces of cane. Beato. **Right:** a postcard of the same.

The Audience Hall of the Deer Throne. Situated on the south side of the palace platform. The steps led to an audience hall which housed the *Me-ga-thana* throne, from where the royal white elephant was viewed by the king on great ceremonial occasions. Beato.

53 Mandalay - တောင်စမုတ်ဆောင်(မိဂါသနပလ္လင်)နှင့်ရေစက်သွန်းပြာသာဒ်တော်

**Chief Commissioner's House, Mandalay with Sir Charles Crossthwaite and
Suite in the Garden.** The Chief Commissioner's house was built over the Se-tha Gate
on the north face of the city square. The long buildings on each side of the central
spire were for members of his staff. Beato.

British Officers on Horseback. Within the City
Wall of Mandalay, c.1890.

Dacoits Captured in the Jungle Near Shwebo. Third Anglo-Burmese War, 1885.
Here a group of Burmans are guarded by Indian soldiers.

Arrival of a Sick Convoy Under the Charge of Surgeon Henderson. Third Anglo-Burmese War, 1885. The building is the official residence of the Shwebo Wun or the governor of the town under King Theebaw. Beato.

Burmese Captives Crucified by Dacoits.
Third Anglo-Burmese War, 1885. Beato.

Mandalay Jail. The spire at the north-west corner of the city walls can be seen in the background. At the time the photograph was taken most of the prisoners would have been rebels, dacoits or freedom fighters. Beato.

**British Officers and Indian Troops on Parade by the Mandalay City
Wall.** c.1890

Above: The Dak Bungalow.
Below: The Hunter.

The Royal School, Mandalay. Run by Dr Marks, it was built mostly with funds provided by King Mindon. The church was consecrated on the 31st July 1873 by Bishop Milman. Many of the older princes attended, accompanied by hoards of retainers carrying gold umbrellas and other paraphernalia. Bourne & Shepherd.

Young Ladies Performing Before Prince Albert Victor at Mandalay. These are young girls of good families who were selected by U Aung Ba, Municipal Commissioner, to dance before HRH Duke of Clarence at Mandalay (26th December 1889). The man seated on the left is the ballet master and behind him are ladies who once attended the royal family. Beato.

The Racecourse, Mandalay. Early 1890s.
The racecourse was situated near Mandalay Hill. Beato.

The Nan-U Hman-se Shwe-kyaung, Mandalay. Known as the 'monastery of gold and glass mosaic', it was situated within the palace. This small monastery was originally built by King Mindon in 1874 and was used by visiting senior members of the clergy. Theebaw went to school there and refurbished the buildings after his accession. After the fall of Mandalay in 1885 is was turned into a church. It is now destroyed. Beato.

Pegu Club — Rangoon.

Royal Lakes, Rangoon.

Elephant working Timber.

Jubilee Hall, Rangoon

Post Card Scenes of Rangoon.

A Burmese Priest.

Lacquered Work, Shwe Dagon Pagoda - Rangoon.

Hpoongyees in tram car returning with alms collected

Post Card Scenes from the Shwe Dagon Pagoda, Rangoon.

The Shwe-nan-daw or Golden Palace Monastery, Mandalay. This was once part of the buildings used by King Mindon and contained the chamber in which he died. His son Theebaw had it dismantled and rebuilt as a monastery in the grounds of the Atumashi Kyaung. It is unusual as it does not have a seven-tiered roof. This wooden building, carved and profusely gilded, is the only surviving example of palace architecture. Beato.

The White Elephant. The picture shows the size of some of the structures used in the cremation ceremonies of monks. They were entirely made of bamboo and paper. This craft is called *sat-pan-hkyi*. Coloured paper lanterns would have been hung from the white elephant. Beato.

Kyaik-Tha-han Pagoda, Moulmein.

Rangoon. River Scene.

Bassein Pagoda.

Bell Pagoda — Bhamo.

Post Card Scenes of Places of Interest.

King Theebaw's State Barge.

Burmese Prince and Princess.

U Khan Dee (Yathee) Mandalay Hill

Monastery near the Atu-ma-shi. This was used as the Officers Mess' of the Munster Fusiliers in 1887. The building is unusual in that there are three seven-roofed spires as opposed to one over the shrine room. Army personnel with their servants can be seen in the foreground. Many monks were turned out of their monasteries and the buildings temporarily taken over by the British Army in 1885. Beato.

The Hman Kyaung. Or 'Glass Monastery'. Built by King Theebaw's Chief Queen Suphayarlat. It acquired its name because of the ornamentation on the balconies is exceptionally fine with glass mosaic work set into carved wood panels. This monastery was often confused with the Mya-taung Kyaung, or 'Golden Monastery', which was commissioned by Suphayarlat in 1885. Late 1880s. Beato.

Burmese Snake Charmers.

Carved stern of a Burmese Boat.

Burmese Buffalo Cart.

Burmese Women, Weaving

Post Cards of Burmese Life.

Burmese Man and Girl.

Enjoying a Smoke

Civilization

Three Monks with Kappiya. A *kappiya* was a monk's lay servant, living in the *kyaung* to earn merit rather than money. The monastery behind is the one that once stood near the Atu-ma-shi and featured on page 72.

Buddha Image Inside the Atu-ma-shi Monastery.
Or, 'Incomparable'. The colossal image contained
compressed royal robes. The surface was lacquered
and gilded and a large diamond set in the forehead
— this was stolen following the disturbances at the
fall of Mandalay. The building also contained the
throne used by Tharawaddy (r.1837-46) father of
King Mindon. Beato.

Above: the Atu-ma-shi. Destroyed by fire in 1892.

Po Sein.

Aung Bala & Sein Tin (Famous Dancers).

Aye Sein (Famous actress).

"Kami Girls" (Beauty and Beast) Arrakan Hill Tribes.

Karen Beauty.

Kachin Girls.

Stupas in the Kutho-daw with Atu-ma-shi Monastery in Background, Mandalay. To the right, the roof of the Taik-taw monastery of the Buddhist Archbishop, and the spire of the East Gate of the Palace. Photographed sometime before 1892. Beato.

The Kyauk-taw-gyi Pagoda, Mandalay. Photographed from Mandalay Hill. In the distance can be seen the city wall and moat, behind to the centre left is the palace complex, to the right is the town. The original three-tiered roof of the Kyauk-taw-gyi was replaced with one of brick by the Sawbwa of Nyaungshwe after the fall of Mandalay. A row of wooden rest houses can be seen behind and to the right of the structure. Beato.

Burmese Cargo Boats on the Irrawaddy.

The Second Defile on the Irrawaddy.

The Fort at Bhamo. The fort, surrounded by an earth wall, housed the British Army, and dates from soon after Annexation in 1885 during the pacification of Upper Burma. Beato.

The Mingun Bell. The largest unbroken bell in the world. It is struck, not rung in the Western style. It hung from a structure made from huge teak logs and bricks. The enormous weight has caused part of the structure it to collapse. A group of nuns can be seen seated near it, in the background towers the Mingun pagoda. Beato.

A Burmese Lady. A studio shot of a 'professional beauty'.

The Beauty of the Village Returning from the Well.
This studio shot shows a 'village maid' dressed in a silk
skirt and velvet slippers supposedly hard at her chores.
Beato.

Devotions at the Arakan Pagoda, Mandalay. The dress of these people suggests that they are wealthy. Five monks can be seen seated by an object covered with an embroidered cloth. Though the particular ceremony cannot be identified, a close inspection will reveal a wealth of detail: curved gilded wands called *kyaing* used in royal processions; sequinned umbrellas; two richly dressed wooden figures. Beato.

Buddhist Abbot Lying in State. The picture shows the body of the Abbot of the Mya-taung Kyaung (Queen Suphayarlat's Golden Monastery) embalmed and covered in gold leaf, resting on his couch and shaded by four white umbrellas.

The Funeral of the Princess of Minelon. As a daughter of King Mindon she merited the white and gold umbrellas seen around the coffin. Other mourners of rank have gold umbrellas held over them. On the right of the picture is the office of the Mandalay Herald Press (later acquired by Beato). c. 1890s. Beato.

မိုင်းလုံမြို့စါးမင်းသမီး၏မသာတော် – *Festivals 90*

A Monk's Cremation. The huge tower which is made of bamboo and tinsel will be burnt. It carries the gilded coffin of a high ranking monk. On the left can be seen a row of Burmese policemen, with their distinctive striped longyis. A British officer dressed in a white uniform and helmet is in charge. Below the tower are five senior monks, the one in the centre is shaded by a gold umbrella. c.1870s. British Burma.

Burmese Dancing Girls. Four young ladies strike a pose. Judging by the amateurish way the hands are held, they appear to be local girls who had been selected to dance before a visiting dignitary.

Left: Arakanese Dancers in front of a processional cart carrying children dressed as the mythological bird man *kainnaya*. c.1870s.
Right: Female Dancers from an itinerant troupe. c.1870s.

Two Young Men with Servants.

A Public Carriage. A group of ladies prepare to go on an outing on a cart called *hle-yin* (dainty cart), because of its light construction and speed. Carts of this type were used for pleasure trips only. Beato.

A Bullock Cart with Hood. Note the solid wooden wheels. Wheels of this design were used for centuries and can be seen in the wall paintings at Pagan and Sagaing. The hood is of woven bamboo matting. Bourne & Shepherd No.2357.

Burmese Public Carriage, Mandalay. King Theebaw and his family were taken in 1885 in a similar carriage to the banks of the Irrawaddy, on their way to exile in Ratanageri, India. Beato

A Burmese Official. He is dressed in a silk *pasoe* or waist cloth and a fur-lined jacket, worn only by the official classes in the days of the monarchy.

A Burmese Princess. A princess and her younger sister are attended by a maid. The princess cannot be identified, but it is likely that she is not of high rank as many of those that were died in the palace massacres of 1879. Beato.

A High Ranking Family. In the foreground mother and daughters sit attended by their maids. Note the fine lacquer receptacles. Beato.

A Burmese Family. The picture shows a family group composed of the father, mother, four daughters, and young son seen at the back left, with long hair and a dark satin floral jacket. Beato [?].

Shan Woman. Beato.

A Shan Warrior. Beato.

Group of Kachins. Note the distinctive Kachin sword in its wooden scabbard. The man on the left is holding a Shan sword, which usually has a thick cord just below the handle. Beato.